Solazzarre, LLC

Copyright © 2018 Chara Rodriguera

ISBN-13: 978-0-9995968-2-1

BREATHE

Sacred Poems and Self Images by Chara Rodriguera

Dear One,

This book is an invitation to slow down and breathe into your heart. These words and images have helped me express and heal the shadow side of myself, as well as unlock my light and pieces of my calling. I hope there is something within these pages that touches you deeply and mirrors back your own beauty, truth and magic.

I chose the title BREATHE because our breath is the most essential aspect of life. It does more than infuse our body, mind and spirit with life-giving vitality. It is a doorway to the present moment and the sacred. It is the greatest teacher and metaphor for the amazing paradox of being human. Just as it takes an inhalation and an exhalation to create one whole breath… it takes giving and receiving, stability and freedom, feminine and masculine, beginning and ending, shadow and illumination to create one whole life.

There are times when darkness obscures our inner light and our understanding of the unlimited creative power we all possess. Thankfully, breath by breath, we can rekindle our inner flame, expand into our full potential and continue awakening to the miracle of being alive.

With Love,

Chara

Poems

Breathe...

and let the magic begin!

The Great Creator

The Great Creator wished for you
imagined you
prayed for you
and then breathed you into life
out of herself.

Like a mother and baby
that are one body at first
and then baby becomes an extension,
a manifestation
of the One.

You are made of the Divine.

That same Creative Spirit is still
this very moment
breathing you into life,
breathing you into full bloom.

Flowers do not bloom on their own.
All of nature's intelligence,
fragrance, beauty and abundance
are infused into the seed
and the entire journey of unfolding.

The seed
and the bloom within it
are an expression of the Great Creator.
And as long as the flower
is connected to its Source
it will continue to blossom
and bring forth all of itself.

As long as you are connected to Source
you will continue to blossom, expand, evolve
and create more out of yourself.

You do not create alone.

You create within the context,
within the relationship
you have with all of life.

You conceive
envision
birth
and bloom
with the Great Creator
as a Great Creator.

Inhale
Exhale

Oh beloved,
I believe you are ready
to finally remember
the heart of your being...
your soul's kite string.

Listen for the yes.
Invite a soft breath
into those tender
lost and forgotten places.
Invite grace to bring morning light
to where it hurts and
where longing haunts you.

It takes courage, my love,
to breathe beyond your flesh
and through the layers of years and life
down into the origin
of the dark and the spark
of everything you are.

Inhale.
Exhale.

Go slow
below the surface
of constructs and business.
Breath by breath
with all your presence
with all your senses.

Be here
for you
and your life unfolding.
Be here
and witness
the power
you are holding.
This is your moment.
Receive it.

Own it.

Inhale.
Exhale.

Today is the day
to understand
you don't have to hide
the destiny inscribed
on the palm
of your own hand.

I know you're afraid
of the nail and the cross
and it seems so much easier to stay small
because
they may naysay
or throw away
your most precious
offerings and confessions.

But small, my darling,
is not who you are destined to be.
Inside you is an infinite ocean,
an invincible sea
that wants to show you
what to do
where to go
which seeds to sow
to grow you into
the universe
you are.

Inhale.
Exhale.

Breathe into your night and day
and the way you love
to receive and give away
kindness like candy.

Breathe into your black and white
and how your passion breaks
through your own clouds
and connects and surrounds
all that is unknown and unmanifest in you
and all that is alive and blessed in you.

You stand between
Earth and sky.
You have the sun and moon
in both your eyes.
You are the one who transforms
yet never dies.

Human and Divinity.
Edges and Infinity.
Shadow and Illumination.
Creator and Creation.

You are the writer
and the fairy tale.
You are the sacred feminine
and the noble male.
You are both sides
and the scale.

Dearest one and only,
you are the search
and you are
the holy grail.

Inhale.
Exhale.

Snowing
Flower Petals

It's snowing flower petals.
It's raining holy water.

I have risen
from a great fall.
I have awakened
from a deep sleep.

Nature is performing her miracles.
I bow down
in awe of her presence
within me
and around me.

There are miracles everywhere.

Stop for just a moment.
Another miracle is here.

We can be part of it.
We can help facilitate it.

Thoughts are medicine.
Words are medicine.
Food is medicine.
Movement is medicine.

Healing is taking place.

Supercharge your heart
and focus on what
you deeply desire.

Life also has a deep desire
for you to be and have and create
all that is in your heart.

But please stop rushing the blossom.

The flower and the sun
know what they are doing.
They know what they are here for
and they do not do anything else.

God's Left Hand

It is said that Jesus
sits in the palm
of God's right hand.

This makes sense to me.
I see why this must be.

Jesus represents
the Divine Masculine.

He is the Christ
the Messiah
the male talisman.

All hail
the right side of the scale.

Royal blood and royal bone
he sits on the yang side of the throne.

But who sits
in the palm
of God's left hand?

Who?

Who?

Who?

I do.

The Divine Feminine
is God's heart.
She balances the universe
with her
music
love
and art.

She is beauty.
She is strength.
She is grace.

She is the sacred
conduit
for life.

She is holy ground.

She is the prayer
and the face
of the Queen Mother.
She is the butterfly
and the moon
illuminating
the sky.

She makes
more love
out of love
and works her magic spells
and she can create heaven
out of hell.

But you will never know
because she will never tell.
Much of her work
is within the womb
behind the veil
beyond your vision
and comprehension.

She is the Goddess
the mystery.
She is the tear
the home
the heartache.

She is the mare
and the dance.
She is the soil
and the plants.

She is the Archangel.

She is the song
that is sung
from the loss of love.
She is the tide
and the bride
and the left wing of the dove.

She is lust.
She is trust.
She is diamond dust.

She is the sweetness
in the juice.
She is all that is birthed
and made brand new.

She is the truth
beneath the truth
beneath the truth.

Who sits in the palm
of God's left hand?

I do.

I do.

I do.

Stand Tall

She stands here
breathing deeply
with tears in her eyes
looking around at her loved ones
who celebrate
all that she is
and all that she is becoming.

She takes a step back
and remembers

all the fear
all the questions
all the struggle
all the desperate wishing
all the while knowing

she was meant for more.

Something truly special
that would allow her to give
and receive
in a way that is divinely hers.

The goddess,
the warrior inside said,

"You can do it!"

And so,
with courageous,
tentative, trusting,
shaky, bold and joyful steps,
she moved forward.

The journey intensified.

The blossoming began.

The yes inside her heart
became bigger than
the fear inside her head.

Now here she stands...

The most full
she has ever been.
The most beautiful
she has ever been.
The most whole, wise, inspired,
purposeful and profound
she has ever been.

How fortunate are we
to see her stand tall
and witness her truth
made manifest.

Incarnations

How deliciously beautiful
and wretchedly painful it is
to live and die many times
within this one eternal lifetime.

How upsetting it is
to grow into your own tree

plant roots
grow limbs
bare leaves
and fruit

just to be chopped down one day
and used as firewood.

I haven't even started grieving
and already I am burning
and required
to be the warmth
for someone else.

It's a mystery, really,
this ongoing transformation.

I want some things to stay the same
and I want some things to change.
I want it to be my version
my vision
of perfection.

Even though I am aware
there is no static
final destination point,
I keep trying.

And all the while I'm trying
life is stirring things up
and presenting me with
more options
more obstacles
more opportunities
and more occupations.

So, I try to find my true self
amongst all this ongoing creation.

And before I can find myself
I have changed again
into something else.

Each time
there is a piece I recognize
and a brand new piece
that reveals itself.

There never seems to be
solid ground to stand on
except the invisible field
that holds up the planets.

There never seems to be
the ultimate me
except the one
that keeps surprising me
saying,

Look at this!

Have you considered this?

Look at what I can do
feel
create
become!

Darkness arrives
and I awaken.
Morning comes
and I wait to be guided.

I sleep.
I rise.
I am born.
I die

over and over

with tears
with triumph
with questions
with the unwavering knowing
that I am the clay
in God's hands

awaiting my next
incarnation.

One Ray
of Light

Who is the messenger
and what is the message
that is powerful enough
to capture your attention?

Who is the voice you will listen to
and trust
when it says you are meant for more…
so much more!

Where is the mirror
that you will allow to reflect
your own beauty, value and unlimited potential
back to you?

What will it take
for you to remember
who you are,
the gifts you've been given,
and the seeds of greatness inside you?

What lightening bolt
has enough voltage
to break these bonds
and jolt your soul back to life?

Which angels
would you believe
when they say,
You are worthy of goodness.
You are worthy of health.
You are worthy of love.
You are worthy of help.
You are worthy to do great things.

You may not know the answers yet.
You may not believe anything new is possible yet.
You may not see beyond the darkness yet.

But you have the power to breathe.
And by inviting one breath in…
you invite
one
small
ray
of light
in.

One ray of light may not be enough
to solve everything
immediately.

But one ray of light
is enough
to awaken your will
and ignite your courage.

One ray of light
is enough
to illuminate
your next step
and the beginning
of a whole new journey.

And step by step
breath by breath
thought by thought
word by word
choice by choice
it is you
who becomes

one
ray
of
light.

Avatar

You already are
more than a star.

Inside you
is an Avatar.

An Avatar is one
who has come
to embody the mystery
of the alchemists
the prophets
and the poets.

Avatars can expand time
and use the power of their mind
to manifest the miraculous.

They are potent and they are just.
They are fierce
and turn everything they touch
into gold.

Avatars are brave
but they are not heroes.
Their job is not to save.
Their purpose is to empower
and mirror back
what is possible.

They are beings of love
and warriors of light.

They spend every day
and every night
whirling up ways
to awaken
hearts
that have been forgotten
or forsaken.

And when fortunes are lost
and beloveds are taken
they are the Earth Angels.

They are living gods and goddesses
who want to introduce the world
to a bigger truth.

They are the mystics
the storytellers
the sages throughout the ages
whose wisdom
is passed down
on the pages
of sacred texts
and in the lockets
of amulets.

You can always tell an Avatar,
not because they talk about enlightenment
or the sacraments,
but because they are the ones
having the most fun.

Inspiration and magic run
through their veins.

When Avatars meet
it is a holy reunion.
The wine starts to flow.
The wind starts to blow
and supporting each other's dreams
is a form of communion.

Avatars are win win.
The embody both yang and yin.

There is no competition.

Their goal is recognition
and to create a community
of divinity
where the main question is
how can we
combine our powers and gifts
to support, create, heal and uplift?

How do you begin
to tap this God force within?

Breathe deeply and fully.
Allow your heart's compass to pull you
toward what is a yes
and everything that will bless
and align you with
higher consciousness.

Know in the core of your soul
that even when you are lost and alone
shattered and tattered
and raw to the bone

flawed
jarred
and scarred

there is so much more
to who you are.

More than human.
More than a star.

Inside you
is an
Avatar.

My Crosses

The cross I was given is

Father, Son, Holy Spirit.

The cross I needed to reclaim is

Mother, Daughter, Holy Spirit.

The crosses I am learning to embrace are

Male, Female, Yin, Yang

Earth, Sky, Sun, Moon

Mind, Soul, Intellect, Wisdom

Matter, Spirit, Finite, Infinite

Stability, Freedom, Structure, Space

Movement, Stillness, Doing, Being

Unknown, Known, Darkness, Illumination

and they all intersect

at the heart.

Gratitude

The noble woman
sits on the doorstep,
steady and content.

She doesn't rush
or quarrel with
the passing minutes.

She doesn't beg
for anything
to be different.

She sits
and breathes in
whatever she can find
to appreciate.

She seems to be
on her own silent quest
of secretly enjoying
being here.

She's not the wealthiest
prettiest
thinnest
or most fashionable.

Yet,
she looks in the mirror and says,
"Thank you."

She always has
enough to eat.
She stands
on her own two feet
and walks anywhere
she wants to go.

She is mesmerized
by the movie
of the ever-changing sky
and every single blossom
catches her eye.

Nothing is taken for granted.

She delights
in turning on the light.
She is in awe
of her fellow human beings
that build towers
pave roads
teach children
and stock shelves in the grocery store.

She is humbled
that she has clean water to drink
and can take a warm shower
anytime she wants.

She is intoxicated
by ripe strawberries, peppermint tea,
spaghetti, rosemary bread
and any kind of chocolate.
Whatever is on her plate is a feast.

When you talk to her,
she affirms you with her eyes.
She gives you her full attention.

She listens
with no judgment
and lets you
finish your sentences.

Your heart will stir
when she says your name
because she pronounces it
with such care
as if you were
the one and only you
for all time.

When you are with her
you will stand taller
because her presence invites you
to own your whole self.

There are people to the
north, east, south and west
creating drama and noise
but she does not let
any person
or external factor
dictate how she will feel
or behave.

No matter what happened that day,
even if surreal
dark
concerning
or frustrating,
she goes to sleep
with a prayer
of gratitude
in her heart
for the adventure of it all
and the knowing
that she is full
of promise
and magic.

I Have Arrived

Today, I am in mourning...
grieving a passing
that no one else can see,
that no one else would understand.

Childhood ideas
teenage wounds
transgressions
that were done to me
and that I have done to myself.

My way of thinking
my way of talking
my view of myself
my view of the world

are just too small.

Like a snake
that has grown too big
for its skin,
I must break out
of this confinement.

And as I have done
many times before
I reluctantly
let go.

I let go
and let life
deconstruct me.

I let go
and let life
recreate me.

As part of
me passes on,
a new part of me
emerges.

Who is this new self?

What is her new purpose?

What is this new me capable of?

I have left the comfort
of my mountain top
and suddenly find myself
tired, weary, tender, raw, naked
and crying on my knees
at the entrance
of a brand new kingdom.

I feel very much alone
and unsure
if my shaky legs will hold me.

But I am determined
to breathe into my new form,
determined to discover
my new magic.

I trust
that I am here
for a reason.

God is with me.

I am ready
to open my new eyes.

Today, I am born again.

I Sit
In A Circle

I sit in a circle
with God
and my guardian angels.

It looks like I'm alone
but I am not.
They tell me it's not my job to fix all this.

Stop trying to fix anything
or anyone.

It's my job to enjoy.

It's my job to see beyond.

It's my job to love
and to make things out of love.

It's my job to be still
and let them teach me...

so they can teach
and create
through me.

They hold both my hands
and look me
in the eyes
and confirm

I can do this.

It will be as natural
as drinking water
and breathing air.

Cry Love

Do you decide to cry?

Or do the tears just flow
as they arrive?

Does the dove decide to fly?

Or do the heart's wings unfold
into the sky?

I cry love.

I cry awe.

I cry tears of liquid Gold.

God is my blood.
God is my bone.
God is my voice.
God is my home.

I don't need to be poor
anymore.

I don't know what all that suffering was for.

It's so simple
like a light was turned on.
I awoke from a dream
and now I see
there is no separation
between the Divine
and me.

My heart is her heart.
My thoughts are his mind.

God's love has infinite faces.
God's love has infinite forms.
God's love has infinite time.

Love can be soft
like the morning light.
Love can be fierce
like a momma bear.

Love stretches me.
Love breaks me down.
Love heals and strips.
Love tears and rips.

Love throws away my royal crown.

Love dismantles what I thought was mine
and leaves me with nothing to name or define.

Love replaces old beliefs with new possibility.

In the past
God was a he.
But now
I believe

God is a he
and a she
and a we.

God is you
and God
is me.

God is all things we can see.

God is all things that have been
and can be.

And so begins the celebration.

Illumination.

Inspiration.

Transformation.

Co-creation!

I breathe God

and God breathes me

and together through eternity

we create.

We create beauty out of love.
We create soul songs and family.

Fear is replaced with faith.
Lack is replaced with gratitude.
Criticism is replaced with understanding.
Negativity is replaced with altitude.

It is clear now
that I'm not done.
I bloom
and I bloom
again and again.

Finally, I trust my opening.

A new glimmer of light emerges
as forgetting awakens remembering,
as the problem stumbles into the solution
and truth tumbles into evolution.

Because this self
and this life
are more than enough,

I Cry Love.

Thank You
For Not
Holding My Hand

I finally found my way

to the mountain top.

I transcended the everyday world
of drama and petty chaos.
I sat high above the breakers
amidst the mantras
that blow by in the wind.

I owned that mountain
and I loved it.
Life was better up there.
Way better.
It was like moving from
a basement apartment
to a penthouse.

I knew exactly how I got there,
so I simply continued the practices
that caused me to levitate.

The sky was my roof top.
Peace and joy were my lap dogs.
I could see everything from that vantage point
and there was little need for me to engage
in the trivial daily wars ensuing in the valley.
That kind of nonsense was for people
and I was something other.

I didn't need to eat.
I no longer needed company
in the typical ways
a human being needs companionship.
I didn't need answers
because there were no questions.

I was not human.
I felt no pain and knew no fear.

I was a beacon, a light house
and those that needed warmth or affirmation
found their way to my doorstep.

I was content with this life,
this purpose.

Then out of nowhere,
glorious day,
my partner found me.
Our babies came
and also joy
insomnia
insanity.

Day by day, inch by inch,
gravity dug its claws into my back,
my arms, my legs, my shoulders, my hands, my feet.

My unwavering buoyancy
kept me afloat much longer
than would have normally been possible.
But eventually my flesh and mind
grew too weary to hold on
and I plummeted to the place
I had spent my whole life climbing out of.

5 Years.

Finally, I was strong enough
to begin my ascension once again.
I knew the feeling I was trying to attain.
I knew the place I was trying to get to.

There.

Where I had once lived in peace.
My mountain top.

Just as I started to feel alive and whole again,
just as I started to climb back up again,
you dug your claws into my back, my arms, my legs,
my shoulders, my hands, my feet.

I was not very strong.
It was easy for you to pull me down.
You said you were there to help me.
But instead you dismantled me.
You tore me apart.

You dragged me through the streets
and let the crowd throw tomatoes at me.
When I pointed to my mountain, you laughed.
You spray painted over my name
and broke the bridge from here to there.

Foolishly, I held out my hand.
You didn't take it.
Foolishly, I waited by the phone.
You didn't call.

Crawling on my knees,
bleeding and begging for any kind of reassurance.

You pointed.

Way over there, beyond the city, beyond the forest.
And I was supposed to get there how???

Crawling?
I hate you!

The gravel in the streets was grinding into my wounds.
It became so painful that I stopped feeling it.
It was so painful that I didn't notice it anymore.

I just kept going.
I must be stronger than I thought.
Ha! I don't need you!
I'm doing it all by myself!

It was like an unending marathon
in which I couldn't see the finish line
but knew which direction I had to go.

At some point,
like an oasis in the desert
I saw it.

My grand entrance.
My golden gates.
My kingdom of all kingdoms.
My castle of all castles.
And yes, right in the middle,
an even bigger, more majestic mountain

with my name on it.

I crawled on my hands and knees.
I pulled myself along on my forearms.
I dug my finger nails into the asphalt
and dragged my ragged body across the finish line.

And there, in that moment
I experienced pure bliss at having arrived.
I experienced pure pride at having done it by myself.

And for a moment,
just a moment...
I experienced pure gratitude
that you did not hold my hand.

I Want

I want to walk with
Jesus, Mary, Buddha, Krishna, Rumi, Aphrodite
on the path of the luminaries
the mystics
the gods and goddesses
who found the sacred
and lived as the light.

I want to sit by the stream
with nowhere to go
eating dates, figs, yogurt and honey
watching the current
teach all of life
how to flow.

I want my aura to create
a fragrance that intoxicates
and inspires
everyone to feel love
see beauty
and create their life
as a living work of art.

I want to bathe
in mineral water, sea salt
and exotic oils
and with a clean, refreshed
mind and body
write poetry by candlelight.

I want to hold my children
closer than my skin,
feel their spirit
touch my spirit
and breathe their innocence
the way I breathe the air.

I want God
to pour all her illuminations
through me
so that my every spoken
and written word
becomes a jewel
on an endless necklace
that makes the world sparkle.

I want to lie down on the grass
and watch my boys
run and tumble
making magic in a land
where there is no time
or threat of anything
other than the stars coming out
to announce their invitation
to dream.

I want my husband and I
to be sun and moon
earth and sky
roots and leaves
in a dance that only we know
that silently intertwines us
within all the different expressions
of giving and receiving.

I want to look in the mirror
into the eyes of my beloved
and really see her loveliness
and cherish her with
attention
acknowledgment
care
and reverence.

I want to give myself permission
to do these things
as it is only I who can do so.

Why should it matter
who I am
where I live
what I have
or do not have?

Why not
say
yes

when yes

is the natural pull
of my heart's compass
in the direction
of all that is beautiful

divine

delicious

affirming

and me.

Alchemy

Inhale love.
Exhale love.

Let love clear the slate.
Breathe away everything you have ever known.
Release all your titles to the wind.

What do you see
when all you see is blue sky?
What do you know
when all you know is no thing?
What guides you
when you no longer have an agenda?
What replaces your belief system
once it has been dissolved
by the glimmer of awakening?

You are the same as you have always been
and you are completely different.
You are the essence of you
and you are brand new.

Like a bellows stokes a fire,
your breath expands and contracts
your rib cage
and your thought process.
It sets your inner flame ablaze.

Pure love creates
heat
that burns off
excess
and illuminates the cavern
of an infinite interior.

Love cleanses.
Love transforms.
Love burns away
the illusion
of self-doubt
and limitations.

Love exists in so many forms.

Whisper in my ear,
what happens when you become
a conduit of love?

Run to me with open arms
and scream your greatest discovery.

You already are
what you have spent
a life-time
looking for.

The Closed Door

How long are you going to look
at that closed door?

Turn around.

There is a grand archway
for you to step through.

There are rockets on your feet
and wings on your back.

You are made for more.

You can fly if you want to.

Yet,
you sit in the mud
crying eternal tears of loss.

You don't see
that the most precious thing
missing from your life
is you.

You have jewels
in your heart
and love letters
still unopened.

You have kingdoms to create
and expeditions to lead.

There are souls waiting for you
to introduce them to the light.

The greatest gift
you will ever receive
is giving the one thing
that only you can give.

But right now
your treasure
has been abandoned
and long forgotten,
buried under the fear
of letting go.

It's time to remember
who you are
and why you are here.

Breathe deeply
into your lungs
and into your body.
Breathe deeply into your heart
and come back to life.

Let all your suffering
give you permission
to be bold and fearless.

Let your suffering
be your key
to freedom.

You've been wrecked!
We all get wrecked
at some point.

It's not pretty or comfortable.
It's not what we would choose.
It's excruciating
and the process
is agonizing.

But life has a savage
and exquisite way
of birthing
divine masterpieces.

You've been through
the hardest part.
You are destroyed.

You can never
rebuild your life
the way it was.

But you do have
all these beautiful pieces
and you do have
the power
to build something new.

Something extraordinary.
Something that reflects
who you are now
and what you are able to give
the world now.

Take a deep breath.

Take your pulse.

Take out an old photograph
of your magical self.

What did that beautiful
beloved child
really want to do and be?

No need for "yeah buts"
at a time like this.

Tell your mind
to shut up for once!

This is your moment to

remember

rescue

and reclaim.

Your life
is in your capable hands.
Your life
is yours to create.

Let your inner child dictate.
Grieve for as long
as you need to grieve.

And when you are ready

turn around.

Walk through the big,
open archway.
Your new life
is waiting for you.

Knowing God
Changes Everything

God used to be an idea,

someone up there watching over us
judging every move
as worthy of reward or punishment.
Something illusive
that required a lifelong search.

But over time

through breath and stillness
through listening and feeling

through loving until my heart broke open
and my conditioning no longer fit

my perception changed.

Expanded.

Now I know God
as the air I breathe.

I know God to be the loving,
eternal, omnipotent, all knowing presence
in
around
between
beyond
all things.

I know God to be the illumination
inside the flame
and the voice
inside my spirit.

I know God to be the poetry
that flows through my soul
and out of my mouth.

I know God to be the white feather
the yellow butterfly
and the red and black lady bug
that catch my eye
causing me to pause and breathe
into the message
that in every moment
in every place
in every creature

God is here.

We can either awaken
and recognize our divinity
or we can sleepwalk
through the habitual rush of responsibilities
and become lost in the turbulent barrage
of endless thoughts, tasks and transgressions,
associating only with the flesh and material world
completely unaware that a bigger
and more brilliant reality exists
just beyond the doorway
of the next breath.

I know God as the creative genius
that has the vision and power
to call into being
whatever a steadfast
and passionate heart beats for.

I know God to be the pillow
I rest my head on,
the flesh that I live in
and the life force
that gives me the calling and courage
to be love in action.

I know God as the eyes
I see in the mirror,
the blessing
of my children's embrace
and the kingdom
we call the universe.

I know God as the ocean
from where all teardrops originate
and the arduous journey of longing
they take to reunite with Source.

I know God as the heat
that softens and purifies me
and the hand that lovingly sculpts me
into a new being.

And because I know this
with everything that I am

life no longer has a beginning
or an end.

Life transforms,
continuously unfolding
into something new
and extraordinary.

Just as the inhale
becomes the exhale
and the exhale
creates a vacuum that summons
the next awaiting inhale...

life is ending and beginning
at the same time.

Life is passing and arriving
at the same time.

Things look different from the mountain top
and that's where I choose to live now.

Even when I find myself in the valley
at night
all by myself

I am no longer so afraid.

I am the mountain top.
So wherever I go
I am home.

I am always home
because I am always with God.

When you know God in this way,
your pain
will not hurt as much.

Your eyes will sparkle
like you know
the greatest secret
that you want to share
with everyone.

You will not fear death so much
because there is no real end,
only transformation.

You will not feel as lonely
because you are never alone.

How could you be alone
when your spirit
is part of everyone
and everything?

How could you be alone
when God is your very
own heartbeat?

Shadow
&
Illumination

We are all
incarnations
of shadow
and illumination.

While we may dwell
in one energy
more than the other,
we are both.

Which one
we associate with
will dictate
how we experience life.

We can live in the basement
or the penthouse.
We own the keys to both.

Heaven and hell
have equal opportunity
to take up residence
in our mind.

Between our shadow
and our light
is an infinite array
of personalities
and possibilities.

Do we not reincarnate
many times
throughout this life,
into and out of titles
roles, definitions, relationships
and levels of consciousness?

Do we not master one area of life
just to find ourselves
a newborn baby in another area?

Are we ever only
a teacher or a student?
Are we ever only
the body or the spirit?
Are we ever only
beginning or ending?
Are we not the breath
and the vessel being breathed?
Are we not always
somehow
excruciatingly and joyfully
both at the same time?

And is it not the shadow
and the light
that create the most beautiful
stories, poetry, music, art
and lives?

Breathe

I used to hide in shadows...

long, extended shadows

passed down from mistreated souls,
as well as the shadows
of my own making.

On some level,
I knew something was very wrong.
On some level,
I knew I was fading away
but my dance with the shadow
was too familiar.

Being entwined
with my tangled tendrils of thought
felt safer than venturing into the sun.

Like a vampire
burned by the light,
I would turn
and curl inward.

A porcelain doll
still in its box.

A paper marionette
without a voice.
A living gossamer ghost
dissolving into the background.

So unaware
of the magical potential
locked inside
my own treasure chest.

And then came the turning point,

the fork in the road
that lead to the two eternal pathways
that each person
must eventually choose.

The first,
the pathway of the shadow,
the tenuous path
of those that stay bound to the past,
bound to the conditioning of childhood
and old wounds
and bound to the imposed limitations
of outside influence.

The second,
the pathway of the soul,
the illuminated path
of those that are brave enough
to reincarnate into a new self
and a new world
of their own creation.

Which would it be?

As I remained frozen with fear
a teacher appeared
and asked me to breathe.

Breathe.

Breathe.

A ray of light entered.

Breathe.

Another ray.

Breathe.

Revealing...Me.

Me
She
We
are so splendid.

I look into the mirror
as if for the first time
and see

A Goddess

A Warrior

A Magician

A Dreamer

A Beauty

A Diamond

A Creative Genius

A Divine Being

A Living Gossamer Angel.

Just breathe.

The shadow now accentuates
the fullness
of my presence.

My attention is forward.

My heart

is unfolding

toward

the sun.

My treasure chest is mine
to share with the world
in any way I choose.

I used to hide in shadows

but now I cast them behind me

as I expand

and step

into

the light.

Breathe...

and live your own
kind of magic!

Gratitude

Thank you to my beloveds Gil, Von and Zan. You give me a million reasons to breathe and smile every day.

Thank you to my loving mother and father, Linda and Louis Calderone, and my beautiful sister, Weezy Jones, for being the best family ever.

Thank you to my dear Inang and Tatang, Tiffany and Ben Rodriguera, my extended family, friends, teachers and students who are my source of support, inspiration and joy.

Thank you to my awesome and talented friend, Casey Sabol, for believing in me and making BREATHE a reality. I am forever grateful to you for sharing your expertise, vision, time and care to make this dream come true.

Thank you to my coach, Nancy Levin, and all my Worthy Sisters who encouraged me to be Fierce, Fabulous and Jump!

Thank you to Cacky Bell, Jeanette Jaworski, Jillian Keller, Kathy Kish and Madelana Ferrara for taking the time and care to offer your supportive feedback.

Thank you to Yolanda Fundora for always rocking the perfect design.

Thank you to the talented friends and photographers who looked through the camera lens with love to help create these special images.

Photography Credits

Cover: Chara Rodriguera (2001)

The Great Creator: Gil and Chara Rodriguera (2017)

Inhale Exhale: Lizzy Sabol and Chara Rodriguera (2017)

Snowing Flower Petals: Gil and Chara Rodriguera (2012)

God's Left Hand: Chara Rodriguera (2017)

Stand Tall: Weezy Jones and Chara Rodriguera (2012)

Incarnations: Zan and Chara Rodriguera (2015)

One Ray of Light: Chara Rodriguera (2012)

Avatar: Lizzy Sabol and Chara Rodriguera (2017)

My Crosses: Von, Zan and Chara Rodriguera (2017)

I Have Arrived: Gil and Chara Rodriguera (2013)

Gratitude: Ed Ajaj and Chara Rodriguera (1995)

I Sit In A Circle: Michel Loewenthal, Anna Heireth and Chara Rodriguera (1996)

Cry Love: Chara Rodriguera (2002)

Thank You For Not Holding My Hand: Tim Corlett and Chara Rodriguera (1997)

I Want: Chara Rodriguera (2001)

Alchemy: Frank Priore, Ed Ajaj and Chara Rodriguera (1994)

The Closed Door: Michel Loewenthal and Chara Rodriguera (1999)

Knowing God Changes Everything: Ed Ajaj, Michel Loewenthal and Chara Rodriguera (1997)

Shadow & Illumination: Chara Rodriguera (2015)

Breathe: Anna Heireth, Michel Loewenthal, Peter Sorfa and Chara Rodriguera (1999)

About Chara: Carolina Rivera (2014)

About Chara

Chara is a Mother, The Creator of Sol Path Yoga and The Optimal and Dream Life Programs, Inspirational Author, Actress and Self as Art-ist.

Since 1995, Chara has been a student and teacher of Yoga, Meditation, Mindfulness and Inspired Living. She specializes in sharing empowering messages and practices that support the process of illumination, transformation and celebration.

Known for her intuitive, poetic and loving style, Chara inspires people all over the world to live their own kind of magic. For more information, offerings and a complementary companion meditation to this book please visit:

Chara.tv

Made in the USA
Middletown, DE
06 June 2018